THE ROSS UNION WORKHOUSE

1836 - 1914

by
C A Virginia Morgan
Joyce M Briffett

Published by the Ross-on-Wye and District Civic Society
Sunnyside, Leys Hill, Ross-on-Wye.
Printed by Herefordshire Council
Hereford

ISBN 0-9532021-0-0

ROSS·ON·WYE·
& DISTRICT

CIVIC SOCIETY

THE ROSS UNION
WORKHOUSE

1836 - 1914

by

C A Virginia Morgan
Joyce M Briffett

PINK PUBLICATION No 11

CONTENTS

Thanks

Location Map

Ross-on-Wye Workhouse Buildings - 1951

THANKS

Thanks for help and information are offered to :-

Our Husbands Mervyn Morgan and Barrie Briffett

Mrs Heather Hurley, Hoarwithy

Mrs Mary Harding

Mrs Sylvia A Morrill, Hereford

Mrs V J Robbins, Weston-under-Penyard (whose parents were Master and Matron
of the Workhouse from 1923 - 1950)

Mr G Brunt, Architect, Messrs Framework, Hereford

Mr C John Powell, Ross-on-Wye

The Staff of the Herefordshire Record Office, Harold Street, Hereford

The Staff of the Libraries in Ross-on-Wye and Hereford

Mr M Morris, previously Editor of the 'Ross Gazette'

Dr Colin D Price of Walford

Map reproduced by kind permission of Mr C John Powell

Key :

Ross Union Boundary —————————

Union District Boundaries —–·—–·—–·—–·—

Parish Boundaries . . . .

ROSS POOR LAW UNION IN HEREFORDSHIRE - 1836

Ross Union also included Lea [Gloucestershire] and Ruardean [Gloucestershire]
and
Aston Ingham and Linton were added in 1894

ROSS UNION WORKHOUSE 1836 - 1929

INTRODUCTION

A new Community Hospital stands at Dean Hill, Alton Street, Ross - this was the site of the Ross Union Workhouse. Many local people have memories of the Hospital that replaced the Poor Law Institute there. This account is part of the story of those who lived and worked in the Workhouse between 1836 and 1914.

Until 1834 and the new Poor Law Amendment Act, the poor were the responsibility of their respective parish. Justices of the Peace decided on the local Poor Rate and this was levied on occupiers of land and property. Parish officials - paid Overseers - were appointed to obtain the funds and, together with the Churchwardens, distribute 'relief' to the needy poor. Stringent settlement regulations, outdoor relief and, in many parishes, a Poor House or House of Industry, were the basic features of the support of the parish poor. However, in many impoverished rural areas, householders were exempted from paying rates and their rents were often subsidised by the parish. Initiative and mobility of labour were discouraged by the Settlement Laws, with labourers surplus in one region unable to seek work in another.

C A V Morgan   June 1994

Dean Hill Hospital, Formerly Ross Union Workhouse

By 1830 the Poor Rate accounted for one fifth of the national expenditure. Resentment, riots and machine burning in many rural areas, resulted in the setting up of a Commission to conduct a nation wide survey. Questionnaires were circulated to every town and country area. The Poor Law Report of 1834 [appendix B2] includes the following questions and answers :-

Q - "What are the classes of manufacturers, workmen or labourers in your Parish whom you believe to be most subject to distress?".
A - "We have no manufactories. I consider that the number of mechanics and labourers are about equal who feel distress". [Mr John Hardwick, Asst Overseer for Ross Town answered]

> A further question elicited the information that - a journeyman mechanic would average £40 pa and - a labourer in 'average employment' for 10 months £18.5s.6d pa, "But in many instances the labourer has a good garden to his cottage, which enables him to keep a pig, that would be worth when slaughtered, £5 or £6". After ascertaining that a

married man's wife could earn 9d per day, and his four children from 6d to 3d per day, the family's annual income could be as much as £30.4s.0d

Q - "Could the Family subsist on these earnings, and if so, on what food?"
A - "That must depend on the price of food".
Q - "Could it lay by anything? And how much?"
A - "No".

Even before the answers were properly analysed, legislation was rushed through in 1834 and the huge bureaucracy of the Poor Law Commission was born.

Parishes within a 10 mile radius of a market town were to combine in supporting a centralised Union Workhouse. The officials manning the house and those dispensing relief in the parishes, were paid out of Union funds and these funds came from all the surrounding parishes.

The workhouse was primarily a haven for those who could not work or maintain themselves because of youth, age, infirmity or incapacity. The poor who would not work and were able-bodied were not encouraged to apply for workhouse entry - indeed the disincentives of hard and repetitive work, a dull [but adequate] diet, restrictive rules and minimum comfort all combined to make the House a last resort. At the same time the New Poor Law sought to discontinue outdoor relief - the able-bodied no longer received it just because they were in need, but if they insisted they could not find work, they were offered a place in the workhouse - the dreaded ' Workhouse Test '. On entry married couples were separated, the sexes segregated and children over seven removed from their mothers. The inmates were not prisoners. If they gave the Master 3 hours notice they could leave as long as they changed back into the clothes they had come in with. However the children [often abandoned as illegitimate or unwanted], the aged the infirm and the mentally handicapped inmates did remain for long periods in these institutions.

The architecture was designed to indicate order, efficiency and confidence in the new social order. The high walls, the forbidding design and the impressive size of the new workhouses proclaimed a regime of deterrence and authority.

'Out-relief', despite the central body's ruling, did continue and from the Minutes it appears that the Ross Union Guardians were generally kindly towards those in need.

ADMINISTRATION AND FINANCE

ADMINISTRATION
The rules for Union administration were clearly laid down by the Poor Law Authority. Boards of Guardians were elected annually, on a restricted property-based franchise. Women and manual workers could not become Guardians until this property qualification was abolished in 1894.

A Master and a Matron were in charge of the running of the workhouse reporting to the Board at their fortnightly meeting. Usually the workhouse was served by a Medical Officer, a Porter, a Schoolmaster, a Nurse and a Curate. The paid Clerk was the linchpin of the Union and he normally had legal training. Out of the House, district based Relieving Officers were responsible for identifying and maintaining the paupers who were not eligible to enter the Workhouse but were eligible for ' out-relief ' - this was in the form of bread, money, clothes and shoes.

The Guardians and the Union Treasurer were Honorary Administrators. Their main aim was to restrict expenditure on poor relief in their areas. The meetings carefully recorded in the 27 minute books detail their decisions. They approved tenders and checked tradespeoples' estimates and invoices. They scrutinised the Master's and Relieving Officer's Day Books and Accounts. They appointed and dismissed staff and debated the claims for relief sent in by paupers. However, the Poor Law Commission had to sanction most of the Guardians' decisions and this often caused tension. While the Guardians wanted to keep the ratepayers' costs down, locally, the Commission wanted to defend itself from criticisms of the new, more ruthless system, nationally.

Within the Workhouse the Master ruled. He ensured that every inmate obeyed the rules - these were usually displayed on the walls of the wards. He saw that the dietary prescribed by the Central Authority was rigorously rationed out to each resident. He conducted prayers; with his wife he supervised the sick and attended the dying. He maintained careful records of all income and expenditure and was present at the regular Board meetings. Any pauper issued with an order for entry into the Workhouse had to be admitted. The Master or Matron supervised the pauper's reception, with a compulsory bath and a change into workhouse clothes. The newcomer was then sent to his or her ward or dormitory.

FINANCE

The initial purchase of the site and the cost of the building completed in 1838 were met by an Exchequer loan and the repayment costs debited to the 30 contributing parishes. The ongoing maintenance and administration costs of the Workhouse and the inmates were considerable. Initially these were met by half-yearly 'calls' on the parish rates based on the average of their respective expenditure over the previous three years. As the regional system consolidated, each parish had its call assessed on the relief, indoor and outdoor, given to its particular poor over the previous half-year. Thus in hard times and bad weather the rate would be higher, with the paralleled difficulty for the ratepayers in meeting the demand. In 1861 the contribution system changed, with property rather than poverty the basis for parish payments towards the common expenses of the Union. In 1865 a common rate was levied on all the parishes in each Union so that the poorer ones were subsidised by the wealthier ones.

The responses to these 'calls' were often delayed. Sometimes the Overseers responsible were fined in the magistrates' courts for late or non-payment of parish dues. Assets such as parish-owned property were sold and the proceeds sent to the Union Treasurer for investment. Subsequent dividends helped to defray parish expenditure. Any personal pension, legacy or savings belonging to a pauper was taken over by the Union Treasurer and used to defray the beneficiary's maintenance costs, while he or she received relief of any sort. Some revenue was raised from work done by the workhouse inmates. Stone broken by the able-bodied men was sold for road building, and the oakum shredded by the women was sold. Pigs were regularly bought and fattened and sold at a small profit. In later years some cost saving was made by vegetable growing on land rented for the purpose.

The salary of the schoolteacher was subsidised by the Treasury from 1848, but the rate depended on the competence of the teacher. One schoolmaster refused to be examined! From 1888, as a consequence of the Local Government Act, the Union Officers' salaries were paid from the County rather than the Poor Rates.

All these systems had to be initiated, supervised and audited. Occasional discrepancies are noted and rectified. The few recorded embezzlements, by Overseers and Collectors to the Guardians, resulted in punishment for the perpetrators. Unfortunately the ledgers and day books are not in the local Record Office. All the regular calls on the parishes are noted in the Minute books, as are the Masters' and Relieving Officers' accounts. Details of the building and repair costs are recorded and the payments and expenses are cross-referenced with the relevant account numbers. The clerical and book-keeping systems must have been very onerous to maintain. The Clerk was responsible for their efficiency and accuracy.

Even without access to the ledgers and account books most of the financial negotiations of the Union can be derived from the Minute books.

BUILDINGS

There had been a smaller Parish Workhouse on the site at Dean Hill, with access to Corpse Cross Street, as it was then called. The land had been bequeathed by Jane Furney in May 1728 for the use of the Parish of Ross, "for ever". A barn stood on the ground, but by 1819 a record of the Benefactions of the Parish Church and the Poor of the House notes "the now Workhouse and garden". In December 1809 James Powles acquired a 99 year lease of a plot of garden ground, part of these premises. The next reference found is in the replies to the 1834 Poor Law Commission queries. One answer records that there were then 18 adults and 5 children living in the Ross Parish Workhouse; the cost per person including clothing, was 3s.3d per week and another 9d each per week covered the costs of the establishment.

After a meeting convened to secure the agreement of the Ross Ratepayers, it was decided that the Workhouse and its land should be sold to the new Union for £500 plus interest at 5% pa.

The Guardians of the Union commissioned Mr Plowman of Oxford as the architect and a tender to build a new Workhouse was accepted from Thomas Tristram of Ross; his figure was £2,200 but with alterations and fees the final cost of the building was £3,650.

The inmates were moved to the smaller Poor Houses at Weston-under-Penyard and Upton Bishop. From this it is presumed that the earlier building was completely demolished .

Delays and problems are listed in the Minutes, but on 2nd January 1838 the newly appointed Master and Mistress, Benjamin and Mary Ann Jeffreys, received 53 pauper residents in the new building designed to accommodate 160. Problems continued: the "warming apparatus" did not function properly. Finally the contractor suggested springs should be fitted on the doors as the inmates habitually left them open! In 1838 the House contained 80 residents and was reported as full. Alterations were made both in accommodation and, in 1839, to allow baking on the premises. This bread was supplied to both the House and to the outdoor poor as their relief.

A well was sunk to such a depth as would ensure -----"a supply of water at all seasons" ----- but this supply was to prove insufficient. Mr John Phipps sent in his estimate for a new pump - [see below]

Drains were a recurring nuisance; in 1840 leave was sought from the Reverend Ogilvie to "drain the fever wards through the adjoining Glebe Garden".

In 1858 a new Dead House was built and the previous one converted as a bathroom for the boys. [Deceased paupers were always taken back to their own Parish for burial].

The Workhouse was proving too cramped and under pressure from the Poor Law Board, the Guardians decided in 1862 to look for a new site for a new and larger building.

However, it was decided to enlarge the existing site and, after much negotiation, in 1868 Glebe land was purchased for £700. Plans were invited for an entirely new Workhouse and five designs were submitted under false names. The Guardians had added the incentive of an award of £40 for the chosen plan. At a special meeting the Board conducted a "minute examination to discover the special merits of each plan". "IDONEUM" was selected and it transpired that it came from Messrs. Haddon of

Minute Book K42/407 p256

Hereford and Great Malvern. In September 1872 tenders were invited for the construction of the buildings, but significantly these were described as alterations and not a new Workhouse. There was reference to Messrs Haddon's plans in the 18th May, 1872 edition of THE BUILDER : they were completed at a cost of "less than £34 per head of inmates and preferably 6 shillings per cubic foot of the entire building".

The lowest tender in the sum of £7,849 was chosen from John Everal of Great Malvern as follows

		£
1.	Principal Building	3,670
2.	Infirmary	1,535
3.	Fever Building	645
4.	Receiving Buildings etc	850
5.	Vagrants' Wards	897
6.	Boundary walls and roads etc	252
		£7,849

Priority was given to the construction of the vagrants' wards, on the north east of the site. These itinerants were always a cause for concern in the neighbourhood, particularly when casual work was scarce. The new buildings increased the size of the Workhouse substantially. As there is no mention of the inmates having to move it is possible that some of the 1836 buildings remained.

In 1874 there is reference to the need to 'arch over' the well in the old Workhouse ----- "leaving a hole for a pump to be put up if hereafter necessary such hole to be covered with a flagstone". The

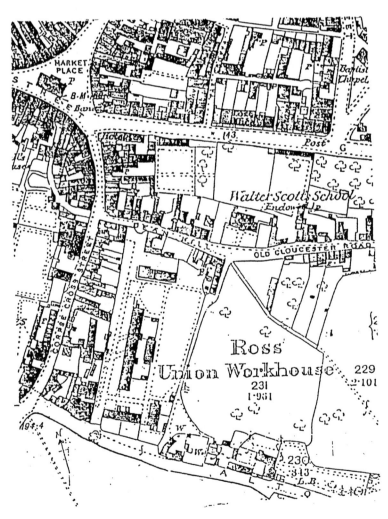

Based on the 1889 Ordnance Survey

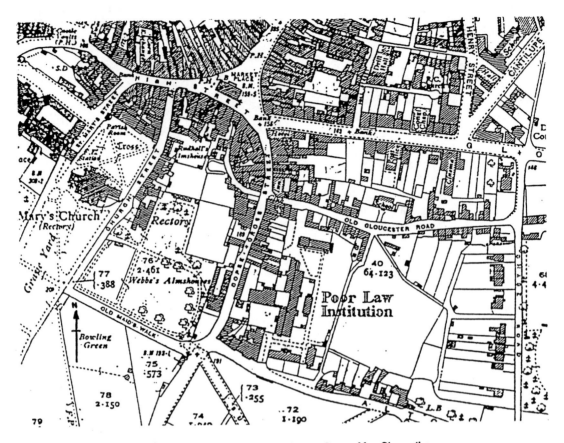

This Revision c1927 of the Ordnance Survey Map Shows the
Significant Extension of the Workhouse compared with the map on page 5.

Architects' reports describe the two entrances, one from Alton street and the other next to Dean Hill. Also the cost of a new wall between the Workhouse property and the property bordering Corpse Cross Street was estimated at about £65, whilst the one bounding the cottage property "which abuts on Dean Hill would be about £30". By February 1874 Mr Everal had completed the work. An interesting order by the Master is his request for 31 pokers and 31 shovels which were required for the different fireplaces in the new buildings. Also 13 galvanised pans for earth closets for the Infirmary and other buildings were ordered from Messrs Perkins & Bellamy of Ross, at 3s.0d each.

But the House was still too small.

Plans were requested from Mr Pearson of Ross for an extension but these needed amendment by the Local Government Board [May 1875]. Despite pressure the Guardians would not agree to further expense and baulked at Mr Pearson's insistence on payment for his plans - he wanted "£36 for them but would reduce this to £25". Heated exchanges in the Board Room led to Captain Power's "desire to resign as Chairman of the Board". One Guardian used strong terms of condemnation of the Board's proceedings ----- "Dishonest, Disgraceful and Dishonourable" ----- in defence of Mr Pearson's position. Eventually apologies were tendered, the plans approved and Mr Pearson instructed to take out the "quantities". He estimated that, if old materials were re-used, the extensions would cost £3,000. But all the tenders were rejected as too costly.

A year later the School Inspector issued a critical report. The School Teacher was overstreched and no progress had been made with the completion of the Workhouse since his last visit. In reply to the Guardian's query Mr Pearson reported ----- "the only buildings that can be erected without interfering with the old part of the House are the wings for the accommodation of the men and women adjoining the principal buildings". In May 1881 it was resolved that a house and buildings in Alton Street adjoining the Stone Yard should be bought and one of the Guardians, Mr Brunsdon, was to offer £150 on behalf of the Board. In 1882 Mr Kemp tendered £45.10s.0d to pull down and rebuild the north-eastern boundary wall.

The House was becoming increasingly overcrowded and in 1889 it was decided that Mr Pearson's plans should be implemented and under his son's directions [Arthur Pearson] tenders were again sought. These included a new kitchen and dining room, but unfortunately the plans have not been found. The architect of the new Community Hospital deduces that the principal spine building was extended on its south-west site. A tender for £4,350 was accepted from Messrs Henry Millward of Leominster and the works completed in 1890. Accommodation was now available for 200 inmates. In 1904 the Board Room was enlarged and improved. It was rented out to local organisations including an Art and Craft Exhibition in 1909. An office for the Sanitary Inspector was rented and a telephone installed in the building. The bake-house was demolished and the bread supplied from a local baker. The new laundry and kitchen was used by schools for laundry and cooking lessons. The Building costs totalled £4,900. New vagrants' wards were completed in December 1911, built by William Bevan for £175; this avoided the need to send 'casuals' to lodgings. In 1904 the Board Room was enlarged. By 1913 the demand for accommodation had fallen and it would have been possible to allow classification of the inmates according to the principle, but not the practice of the 1834 Act. An article in the Ross Gazette of 14th May, 1914 reports a Poor Law Conference in West Malvern where the difficulties of implementing classification were discussed.

A summary from a Survey by the Royal Commission on the Historical Monuments of England [1994] details the site:

"The site is small and irregular and the buildings were erected close together. To the west of the main entrance on Alton Street were the administrative offices and receiving wards: to the east were the infirmary and fever wards. The main building, in the centre of the site, followed the corridor plan which was favoured for workhouses throughout the country between the 1840s and the 1870s. To its west was the dining hall, kitchen and laundry, to its east was a schoolroom and to the north a casual ward block".

The land comprising the Workhouse premises was assessed for valuation purposes in April 1914 -

Acreage - 2 acres 29 perches	Original gross value	- £14,746
	less Tithe	- £3
		£14,743
	Original assessable site value	- £ 1,035
	Therefore Assessable Site Value	=£13,708

With all the rebuilding, alterations and extensions, it is estimated that over £16,000 of Union funds was expended on the Workhouse buildings. This was in addition to at least £1,800 on land purchases.

Between 1913 and 1992 the Workhouse changed its name and function. From 1830 to 1834 it was the Poor Law Institution, renamed the Public Assistance Institution until 1943 when it became the Ross Social Welfare Institution. In 1948 it was called the Alton Street Hospital, and more recently the Dean Hill Hospital. Local people used to call it the 'Spike'. This is a colloquial name for a casual ward; to sleep in the Workhouse was to go 'on the Spike'.

In 1976 there was a total of 113 beds. A maternity ward with 4 beds was situated above the Receiving Ward. Lilac ward accommodated the long stay Age Care residents, and Holly and Oak wards the female and male adults with learning difficulties. A physiotherapy unit and administrative offices occupied the building where the Guardians met so regularly. Only this building remains, as illustrated in the photograph opposite, taken the day before the construction of the new Community Hospital began.

MEDICAL RELIEF

The licensed 'Medical Gentlemen' contracted by the Board of Guardians were required to attend all the sick paupers in the Union, usually by referrals from the Relieving Officers. The Union supplied basic medicines but unusual items had to be bought in. From 1865 to 1868 a dispensary was opened at the Workhouse with a qualified dispenser, Mr John Cotton: the Medical officers' salaries were reduced by "10£ per cent" and, in a later entry, "the Board would supply bandages, leeches and syringes where ordered by the Medical Officer" (MO). In 1875 Mr Kemp was engaged to convert the Register Office to a dispensary but later there were many complaints as the Dispenser was frequently absent and, in one case, a women had walked from Llangarren for her medicine. The local chemist benefited ----- in April 1878 the Guardians chide the Dispenser to "keep up his stock of drugs so far as is consistent with proper freshness so as to render it unnecessary to make purchases in the

Town". Mr W S Rootes and Mr C E Thomson were the first Medical Officers, with the Union divided into two districts. When the Union House opened in January 1838, Mr Thomson took on its care at a salary of £15.0s.0d. Until 1842 the MOs were paid on a contract basis and their charges in 1839 were:

For every single case within 2 miles of Ross the charge would be 5s and beyond that distance 7s.6d
For all Family cases within 2 miles of Ross 7s.6d and beyond that distance 8s.6d
For all midwifery cases 8s.6d
For all fractures and dislocations and for amputations and operations for hernia £1.1s.0d

From 1839 Edmund Jones was appointed MO in charge of the Workhouse and his kindly service ended in 1863 with the Guardians' tribute to his "assiduity and attention to his duties". He was also the Public Vaccinator, earning 1s.6d for every successful case, but since many people did not return for checking on the seventh day he often worked for nothing.

C A V Morgan   October, 1995

Smallpox is first mentioned as prevalent in August 1838, and the Master was told to have all the children vaccinated. In 1840 Mr Jones undertook to visit all the out-paupers on specified days at Old Gore, Hope Mansell, Llangarren, Hoarwithy and Ross. He had to keep "two books one of which would note the residence of every person successfully vaccinated" and give them a certificate. The Poor Law Board issued frequent directives, and later on proceedings were taken against parents who did not allow their children to be vaccinated. Through their relative isolation the inmates of the House were protected, but in May 1859 John James of Goodrich was admitted "suffering from smallpox". The overseer responsible was criticised as the Guardians said the case was "not one of sudden and urgent necessity".

Other infectious diseases are reported, outside, and the use of a fever ward was recommended to cope with any sudden influx of sick paupers. In the early years Mr Jones' concern about the severe diarrhoea prevalent in the House led to his report to the Board - "although this complaint has and usually does prevail in the Autumn in all places yet in the Workhouse it had been much aggravated and increased by the unwholesome nature of the atmosphere created by the present method of warming three of the wards which, while the temperature consistently varies, tends neither to ventilate nor purify the air as a common fireplace does which in my opinion would prevent the present close and disagreeable smell and great deposit of water upon the doors and walls".

After the considerable extension of the Workhouse in 1874 the MO, Dr Thomas Jones, told the Board that "the newly erected infirmary and infectious wards are ready for occupation" and 'the Master was directed to avail himself of the extra accommodation at his disposal'. But the fever ward was only used once, until 1909, when nine children and the Matron were taken ill with scarlet fever. In 1912 six children were isolated there, suffering with scabies. In 1884 water closets were substituted for the earth closets in the Fever Ward.

The 'itch' was a problem: in 1856 Mr A Willmott, the House MO, had to report on the number of such cases. He said it was on the decline and "expressed the hope that it would soon be good rid of entirely". One four year old child contracted the itch whilst in the House but the Board decided to discharge his mother to go into service and "to keep the child in the Workhouse until he could be cured of the disease without compelling his mother to remain with him in the House".

The Board paid a subscription to the hospitals they used, and an application for one was received from the newly established Eye and Ear Hospital, Hereford, in November 1883. Much care and cost was given to the disabled, the blind and the deaf and dumb paupers. One boy, Samuel Hodges of Ross was sent to the Deaf and Dumb Asylum, Old Kent Road, London for board and instruction and in March 1861 he became an apprentice to Mr Joseph Evans of Ross - Basket Maker --- with the Board arranging the indenture payment and also "to supply his fit out".

Many single expectant pauper mothers came in to the House to have their babies and had to occupy the same room as the mothers who were lying in. It appears that mothers could look after their infants, but there were sad cases of desertions.

A nurse was employed for most of the period but there was a remarkable 'turn over' in the job, with at least eighteen in the post between 1838 and 1914. Sometimes there were no answers to the advertisements and the Matron had additional work, but----- "thus the salary and rations of a nurse were saved". An inmate applied for the post once, but as she could not 'read writing' she could only act as assistant to the Matron at a salary of £10.0s.0d pa, subject, as were all decisions, to the sanction of the Poor Law Authority. Another nurse was summarily dismissed for 'insubordination' and the porter resigned at the same time. In 1898 it was resolved that dying and bedridden patients were to be removed from the sick ward and a hospital trained nurse was appointed

The Guardians were consistent in their efforts to save ratepayers' money. An example is the Minute in January 1850 ----- "Dr Jones applied for the payment of a fee of one guinea to Dr Barratt for assisting him to amputate the thigh of a pauper in the workhouse. The Board, considering that all such expenses were paid by Dr Jones' salary, felt necessitated to reject the application". At this time Dr Jones' salary as MO for the Workhouse was £25 per annum, and he earned a further £60 as MO of one of the Districts. There were generous Guardians. Mr Hall at his request was permitted 'to erect at his own expense a pole etc in the yard for the boys in the Workhouse to exercise themselves in gymnastics'.

After the Public Health Act of 1872 a Medical Officer of Health should have been appointed for the whole Union "including that portion of the parish of Ross under the supervision of the Ross Town Commissioners". The salary was to be £70 per annum, and an Inspector of Nuisances was also to be appointed at an annual salary of £60. But the Guardians hesitated; they wanted to see what other Unions were doing!

Initially the water supply was from the well, later it was obtained from the River Wye. Fortunately for the health of the inmates an 'unlimited and always consistent supply' of spring water was laid on from Mr Turnock's property, Merrivale, in 1879.

It was ironic that the Urban Sanitary Authority had to report a nuisance at the Workhouse arising from a cess-pool. The proposed solution was ----- "could an outlet be obtained into the town sewer running down Corpse Cross Street?"

FOOD AND DIET

The 'less eligibility' test for Workhouse entry required that the diet for those receiving 'inside' relief should not be better than that available to the lowest paid employee outside. The Central Authority drew up different Dietary Tables and the one chosen by the Guardians had to be strictly followed and copies printed "in large type and hung up in the most public places in the Workhouse". Dietary No 1 was initially selected for the adults, but was replaced by one recommended by Mr Cary Cocks. This applied only to the able-bodied adults. The diet for the aged and the sick was unchanged.

"Dietary for able-bodied Men and Women

		Breakfast		Dinner							Supper		
		Bread	Gruel	Cooked Meat	Bacon	Potatoes	Soup	Suet Pudding	Bread	Cheese	Bread	Cheese	Broth
		Oz.	Pints	Oz.	Oz.	lb.	Pints	Oz.	Oz.	Oz.	Oz.	Oz.	Pints
Sunday	Men	6	1½	5	1						6		1½
	Women	5	1½	5	1						5		1½
Monday	Men	6	1½			1½					6	1½	
	Women	5	1½			1½					5	1½	
Tuesday	Men	6	1½	5	1						6		1½
	Women	5	1½	5	1						5		1½
Wednesday	Men	6	1½		2	1					6	1½	
	Women	5	1½		2	1					5	1½	
Thursday	Men	6	1½	5	1						6		1½
	Women	5	1½	5	1						5		1½
Friday	Men	6	1½					14			6	1½	
	Women	5	1½					12			5	1½	
Saturday	Men	6	1½						8	2	6	1½	
	Women	5	1½						7	2	5	1½	

Minute Book K42/407 p 323   1.6.1840

The children under 9 had a different diet:

5 - 9 Years		1 - 5 Years		Under 1 Year	
Bread	8 oz	Bread	7 oz	Bread	6 oz
Meat	4 oz	Meat	3 oz	Milk	? pints
Cheese	1 oz	Cheese	1 oz		

However in 1857 the Medical officer for the Workhouse altered their diet -----'with a view to remove the scorbutic disease which exists among them'.

The aged and infirm had extras like tea, sugar and butter. In 1858 the Master told the Board that all the able-bodied paupers and children over nine years of age should have a pint of milk and water at suppertime. But the vagrants did not fare so well.

The question of the Vagrants Dietary was brought
before the Board; and it was resolved that their
Dietary should be as follows viz:

Supper

Males above 15 years of age	8 oz of Bread
Females Do Do	6 oz of Bread & 1 pint Gruel or Broth
Children 7 to 15 years	Do Do
Children under 7 years	4 oz Bread & 1/2 pint Gruel or Broth

Breakfast

Males above 15 years of age	6 oz Bread & 1 pint Gruel or Broth
Females Do Do	
Children 7 to 15 years	} Same as Supper
Children under 7 years	

Minute Book K.42/419 P883   10.3.1879

Parsnips were ordered by the hundredweight [cwt], onions by the peck or bushel. Oatmeal came from Scotland in 5 cwt supplies [avge price £1 per cwt]. Land at Ashfield was leased for vegetable cultivation, and in 1895 the Royal Cross Estate, opposite the Workhouse, was bought on the understanding that it should never be built on: until the 1960s it was cultivated productively. Tenders for potatoes occur frequently in the records, but in 1846 and 1883 crop failures led to difficulties :--- "it appearing that there was great difficulty in obtaining potatoes, it was resolved that rice and other vegetables should be use alternatively with potatoes as a temporary expedient". Meat was supplied mainly by one contractor : he was very indignant when, in 1872, Australian beef and mutton, at 6d per lb, was ordered from Mr J Hill the grocer. Earlier there was official criticism of the diet for the feeble minded : "the meat is always boiled".

The Local Government Board, in an attempt to improve health standards, suggested that fish be tried :---" the inmates to have 8 oz of cooked fish each, on Saturdays". It was not a success. The Master reported that ---"in many cases the inmates would not touch it and that on the second occasion he had cut up a cheese and given it in lieu of fish. It was resolved that fish dinners be discontinued".

Bread was the most important item in both inside and outside relief. From May 1839 until March 1890 it was baked on the Workhouse premises, and the succession of bakers, [sometimes assisted by the lads in the house] earned £1 per week --- later augmented by 1/6d per week for every sack [280 lb] of flour over 12 sacks, baked per week. The bread was taken to the 'outstations' by the contractor in his bread cart; in September 1883 the list of outgoings includes :- "H. Digwood paid for conveyance of bread 17s.0d per wk. Conveyance of dead 3s.6d per journey". Years earlier the Guardians, always parsimonious, thought the bread delivery costs too high and invited tenders " for the construction of a light sprung wagon with covered top capable of holding about 320 loaves of bread". However the project was too expensive and the bread deliveries contracts continued. The 4lb loaves cost between 4d and 10d each, for the purpose of parochial reimbursement, and they were marked with an indented R.U. Regrettably the Relieving Officer for the vagrants was suspected of cutting this mark off the bread and selling the loaves : he was dismissed. Quality control was practised by the Board, from samples produced from each tender. In one case the Workhouse Baker blamed his poor product on the flour. The contractor, Mr J B Whittard [of Whitchurch], indignantly responded by arranging for his employee to bake in the Workhouse with his flour and the usual barm (used instead of yeast). An "excellent loaf was produced therefrom" and the Workhouse Baker was "censured and cautioned".

Restriction of food as used as a punishment, but never with children, nursing mothers or the aged. Wine and brandy were frequently ordered from Mr Purchas of Ross. The auditor criticised the Master, in 1872 for the quantity of brandy used. He had an unusual explanation. It had been ordered by the Medical Officer to be given to the Nurse as there had been an "inmate of one of the wards with frost-bitten feet and the toes gradually decayed and fell off, the effluvia from the sores being so offensive that the Nurse could not discharge her duties without stimulants and the brandy referred to above was given to her". A résumé of indoor costs compiled in 1914 notes that in 1904 - 32½ gallons of whisky and spirits were purchased whereas for the year ending 31.3.1914 - 2½ gallons only.

Reproduced by kind permission of Mrs V J Robbins   c1930s

<u>Christmas Day at the Workhouse</u>

As the years went by the diet became more varied, and more generous. Tea was available to the inmates generally but it was weak! ----- "ordered that 1 oz of tea be used with 8 pints of water ----- instead of with 10 pints of water as hitherto". The diet for the officers was more liberal than that of their charges. Sir E W Head, the Assistant Poor Law Commissioner, in March 1838, recommended that rations "as for seven should be allowed for the Master, Matron , Nurse and School mistress!" All the officers had a beer allowance, or they could be allowed " three halfpence a day in lieu".

But there were good times. Following the tradition of a good Christmas dinner being provided by public subscription in Ross Parish one of the founder Guardians, Nathaniel Morgan, proposed that this should continue. A dinner of roast beef and plum pudding was given to all the inmates every year on Christmas Day.

An entry for December 1879 reads ----- "the usual dinner to be provided to the Inmates of the House on Christmas Day with exception of bad characters who may come in immediately". On Christmas Day 1909, the whole day's fare is noted:

Breakfast :Bread 8 oz. Butter 1/2 oz. Tea 1 pint and milk and arrowroot per sick dietary.
Dinner   :Cooked meat, vegetables and Christmas Pudding with one pint of Ale or
                                                                mineral water.

Supper	:Bread 6 oz. Butter 1/2 oz. Tea 1 pint and 4 oz. Sultana Cake.
Extras	:Male Inmates - 1 oz. tobacco each
	Female - 2 oranges
	Children - oranges and sweets.

Other special occasions were celebrated with 'good dinners' : the Central Board sent a circular to all the Unions, sanctioning a change in the dietary on Her Majesty's Coronation, her Marriage and her Jubilee. At the Coronation of King Edward VII the diet was :

> Cold Meat, pickles, salad, fruit tarts
> Beer and ginger beer for men, also tobacco
> Tea and sugar for women

Towards the end of this period, with growing awareness of nutritional requirements in a balanced diet, those in the Workhouse were probably better fed than their friends and relatives outside.

CHILDREN

The children in the Workhouse came in with their destitute parents, or were brought in on their own to relieve the financial pressures on their families. Many children were born in the House and sometimes they were abandoned there. The rules in 1847 dictated : "so long as any mother is suckling her child she ought to have access to it at all times except when she is at work, and the child ought not, even then, to be completely beyond the mother's reach". Children under seven could sleep in the female wards. After seven according to the classification system, the boys and girls were separated, sleeping in male and female dormitories.

Outside the House there were complex rules for the different pauper children's needs. In the early days widows, and deserted or separated wives, could have relief for their children under 7, and the authorities could not remove those children. After 7, if her case was justified, a mother could send the child into the Workhouse without accompanying it.

Nationally in 1838, in the Workhouses of 478 Unions sending returns, there were : 42,767 children under 16 - 44% of the total Workhouse population. In 1840 this number had risen to 64,570 of whom 56,835 were between 2 and 16.

Relief was allowed to illegitimate children under 16, and this was deemed relief to the mother as long as she remained unmarried or a widow. But discrimination against such children is recorded. In 1866 an illegitimate little girl was being nursed by a Mrs Griffiths. She had complained already to the Board that when the child had a fever the District Medical Officer had refused to call. He had rationalised this, when summoned before the Board, saying he believed the child ----- "was suffering merely from a cold and that he did not feel justified in attending illegitimate children without a special order". The case worsened. Mrs Griffiths applied for out-relief for her charge, but, following the rules, ----- "the Board refused ----- but, as the mother had deserted it, consented to take the child into the Workhouse." The putative father, who worked at the Royal Hotel stables, was ordered to pay 1s.6d weekly towards the child's maintenance.

As late as 1905, when 'boarding-out' of Workhouse children was regarded as a better upbringing than that within an institution, illegitimate children of able-bodied women in the Workhouse were not included in those to be selected.
There are many references to the Clerk's attempts to coerce fathers into supporting their offspring. On one occasion he was directed "to see the women now in the Workhouse and ascertain whether there was sufficient evidence to enable the Guardians to obtain Bastardy Orders upon the alleged children of their Putative Fathers". The next meeting reports developments. In one case ----- the Clerk reported that the child had died, and that "thus there was an end to the case"; with the second woman -----" there was no corroborative evidence on which to obtain a summons against the alleged putative father of the child".

In the last case -----"the mother was to be removed to the Parish of her settlement".

A particularly poignant example of the distress of poverty is the offer of a reward of £1. "to any person giving such information as shall lead to the apprehension of the person who left a child about 5 weeks old at the door of the house in Smallbrook ----- whereby it became and is now chargeable to the Union".

The children in the Workhouse were better educated than many of their fellows outside. As early as 1839 the Master was told to provide the schoolroom with 6 slates and pencils for the use of the children under the Schoolmistress's care and the chaplain (Mr Brasier) was to be requested to order "what books may be wanted for the children's use". Mr Thomas Blake was the schoolmaster from 1848 to 1853, and his list of articles required included a Desk. The Guardians dispensed with the desk request, but said he could "procure books etc from the British and Foreign School Depot" ----- at a cost of £5. Later maps of England and Palestine, and a Tuning Fork, were purchased. A grate was fitted in the schoolroom, a clock was supplied and in 1874 the Clerk was asked to thank Mr F Cooper, who had written on behalf of subscribers presenting a harmonium 'to be used in the Workhouse School'. School inspections were generally satisfactory, but in 1876 it was reported that there were 58 children in the school, of whom 30 were boys, too many for the school mistress to manage.

J M Briffett   1976
The Children's Ward

Industrial training was introduced. This was part of the central policy and the aim was to teach practical skills. The girls were instructed in cooking and household tasks, the boys in manual and horticultural work. At one stage the baker was enlisted as the Industrial Trainer and lads in the bakery were useful assistants. For a short period some children over 7 were sent to Hereford Industrial School at a cost of 3s.0d per week each. With the introduction of compulsory education, from 1874, the children outside the House had to attend school. Indeed the Guardians had to pay their school fees (usually 3d per week) and later children of non-paupers were entitled to have their school fees paid by the Union. But there was some discrimination: the Local Government Board told the Guardians they had no authority to pay the Ferry Toll for non-pauper children going to school!

From 1846 grants had been available to pay the salaries of qualified schoolmasters and mistresses, but two years later these were graduated according to the teacher's proficiency in the classroom. Some Guardians in other Unions objected --- "to teach writing and arithmetic to pauper children was to give them advantages superior to those of the children of the independent labourer". The first schoolmistress, in 1838, was the ex-matron of Ross Workhouse, Mrs Mary Griffiths. She was directed to "walk out with the children when the weather is sufficiently fine" for set times and "to put the children always to bed". After she resigned in 1839, there was a succession of seventeen single teachers. the annual salary was £25 with full board, lodging and washing. Some elected to have "three halfpence a day in lieu of beer". In January one year the mistress was blamed because, it was alleged, she had "not properly attended the children and had allowed their feet to become very sore from chillblains". At the next meeting her resignation was reported. Subsequently, her successor "sent two letters of an objectionable nature to the Nurse and Matron so she is expected to resign". When the schoolmistress left in 1892 it was resolved not to fill the vacancy, and the children attended the Board School. The Industrial Trainer was to look after them out of school hours and the Cook was appointed to the post. By 1905 there were only 6 children to be so instructed, so the post was abolished. Boarding-out of children over 3 was recommended and in 1911 sixteen children were sent out to foster-homes

The Central Authority always had the goal of giving the children of the poor a good start in life. With this aim they often had to persuade the Guardians to spend Union funds. Ross Union seems to have been generous and caring in its responsibilities to the young.

Physically handicapped children were sent to specialist homes, orphans were sent to the Orphans' Home at Leominster and Müller's orphanage in Bristol. When young mothers left the house with their children, their requests for clothes or shoes were usually granted. In February 1862 one eloquent entry reads ----- "Clerk to ask for sanction of Poor Law Board about the proposed allowance of a suit of clothes to the value of £1.5s.10d to George Meek an able-bodied Pauper chargeable to Weston-under-Penyard on his leaving the Workhouse for the purpose of procuring his own living. He has been in the Workhouse nearly all his life and consequently has no clothes of his own". At the next meeting the letter of sanction was read.

When the boys reached the age of 12 they were employed or apprenticed. Despite the Central Authority's reservations about apprenticing children, except for physically disabled youngsters, Ross Union both arranged and supervised many such commitments. One boy, aged 14, was apprenticed to a plasterer in Ross, another to a tailor, another to a basket maker in Linton. In these and many other cases, the term, the premium and the wage to be paid (or invested in a Savings Bank) is detailed. In 'binding' Henry Bell King, a deaf and dumb boy, the Guardians required the Relieving Officer to attend before paying the second moiety of the premium. They "expressed their satisfaction at the progress of the lad" and authorised the payment. Domestic service was the usual employment for girls. A certificate as to their fitness was obtained from the medical officer and agreements were prepared and signed. The boys and girls were usually given an outfit before leaving the House. In one case the girl was to be paid £3 per annum; in another 1s.0d per week. When one of the schoolmistresses retired she applied to take a girl orphan inmate for 12 months as a domestic servant. One girl returned to the house after only 6 months service with a family. She complained that she had been ill-used, the mistress having thrown a bucket of pigs' wash over her. The employer did not deny this and said that she had thrown 3 bowls of whey over the girl who was very 'saucy'. The Guardians did not pursue the matter but demanded the 6s.8d due as wages to the girl, which was put to the credit of the Union.

A few treats are described; in June 1851 all the children in the House were taken to a Railway Fete held on Ross Cricket ground. There was a proviso -----"8 tin dishes be lent for the purpose of the Fete .Mr Minett (the Clerk) undertaking they will be safely returned". In 1865 the Poor Law Board refused to allow payment of travelling expenses of 5s.0d each for three unsuccessful applicants for the post of schoolmistress. The Guardians made a collection between them and — "as there remained 9s.0d the Clerk was directed to hand this over to the Master to provide a treat for the children in the Workhouse".

As with the aged, the policy with regard to children in the Workhouses became more lenient. A circular in 1891 sanctioning newspaper and book purchases for the older people stated that toys could be bought for the children. From 1901 birth certificates recorded the address as 3 Alton Street. Where children were boarded out regular checks on their health and happiness were made by members of the Special Ladies Committee as well as the Medical Officer. Only children under 3 remained in the Workhouse nursery , with the exception of 'ins and outs'; the term for temporary inmates. The rates increased with this more liberal attitude, from 3s.10½d in the £ in 1904 to 4s.6½d in the £ in 1914. The outlay in boarding-out was blamed, as foster-parents received 5s.0d each per child, much more than pauper parents received for out-relief for each of their children.

With hindsight the benefit to the children can be imagined. They had escaped the numbing boredom of an institutionalised life, where there was no challenge, no room for initiative and no future. The Workhouse had been a refuge, but they had to live in the real world.

THE ABLE-BODIED

This classification differed between those living outside and those inside the Workhouse. Outside it defined those able to be, or in, employment. Able-bodied males were aged between 13 and 60, able-bodied women between 16 & 60, all of whom were not mentally or physically incapacitated.

Outside relief was not to be offered to the able-bodied: if they were out of work and destitute, their only relief was to be in the Workhouse. The Poor Law Central authority believed that this would incite all able-bodied people to find work and subsistence without burdening the Poor Rates.

In Ross Union, many exceptions to this rigid rule are recorded in the Minute Books. Examples include a machineman earning 2s.0d per day, when he could work, with 5 children, none able to work ----- he was granted "a pair of trowsers value 8s.6d". A widower with 8 children , the youngest only 14 days old, earning 8s.0d per week asked if the baby could come into the Workhouse as he was sick. As his illness was considered to be only temporary this was granted. In the severe weather of February 1888 an able-bodied man in Goodrich was granted relief, for two weeks, of 3s.0d and 12lbs of bread, value 1s.0d per week. A non-settled pauper, living in Westbury Union had been receiving 4s.0d per week, paid by them but debited to the Ross Union. On the death of the pauper's wife the Ross Clerk wrote to the Westbury Clerk suggesting that the 'pay' should be reduced to 2s.6d per week - this was agreed. As mentioned able-bodied women had to come into the Workhouse if their husbands were ordered in. Single women, widows with children, deserted mothers and mothers of illegitimate children were, if they were able-bodied; given out-relief according to their needs. There were some restrictions on the period of time that this could continue.

The value of the relief was in the ratio of one third bread (or kind) and two thirds money (or pay). Medical relief, if prescribed by the Medical Officer, could be meat, milk or wine. A query was directed to Dr T J Jones, MO for St Weonards District as to the large quantities of wines and spirits ordered in May 1888. In cases of desertion rewards were offered for the apprehension of the errant parents and their names and description were published in the Poor Law Gazette. In 1851 the Master was asked to prepare a list of all the children in the House deserted by their parents, or without parents. The refrain that follows the details of each case is -----"and leaving them chargeable to the Parish of ----- ."

Reproduced by kind permission of Mrs V J Robbins   c1930s

The Master, Matron, Porter, Cook and Nursing Staff

Sometimes the fathers enlisted, but they were traced. One such deserted boy, left in the Workhouse, posed a problem with regard to his settlement. After extensive enquiries ----- "the Master was directed to take the lad to Cardiff and the Clerk to allow the cost of his journey". A reward of 10s.0d was offered to apprehend a delinquent husband: he was caught and sent to Hereford Gaol for three months. A year later the reward was £2 for information as to a desertion of his wife and children, with out-relief ordered for the children as "they are within the age of nurture". In bastardy cases, too, putative fathers were relentlessly pursued, where there was sufficient evidence to convict them.

In all the circumstances, after the first distress of destitution had been overcome, the able-bodied men and women in the Workhouse must have been very restless and the authorities provided hard and repetitive work as a means of avoiding disturbances.

The tasks would have included for the men, care of the pigs (whose profitable sales are frequently recorded), vegetable growing in the allotments rented from Messrs Collins(1862) and later in the land opposite the House. Also wood chopping, stone breaking, water carrying (this in 1855, perhaps due to the frost), and on one occasion, "painting the woodwork in the House and Mr Turnock (a Guardian) to get the paint". The 1914 Minute Book records several cases of 'house labour' employed in decoration and minor repair work. The able-bodied women, when free from care of their young children, would have to do all the chores of the large establishment. The House could hold up to 160, but after the extensions the maximum accommodation increased to 200. The mending may have been unsatisfactory because an entry in 1882 reads - "Resolved to appoint a tailoress to repair inmates' clothes - to be paid wages with rations".

On entry to the House the paupers were taken into the separate receiving wards, bathed and given workhouse clothes (their own were kept to be returned on discharge). They were examined by the House Medical Officer, classified and shown to their stark quarters. In the evenings it was dim in the wards because although Mr Harris, the proprietor of the Ross Gas Works supplied metered gas to the 'new' Workhouse in 1873, the Guardians "struck out fifteen of the proposed lights" !

As the Minute Books only record routine administrative and management procedures, they are enlivened when accounts of misbehaviour and the consequences are described. In all these predicaments the Guardians were anxious to conform with the rules and regulations of the Central Authority.

There are several reports of boys and women absconding - but the censure is greater when the escapees are in Workhouse clothes as this was theft. A woman had a bottle of brandy hidden in her clothes when admitted. Some of the younger women's names recur, either for refusing to work or being insolent. The usual punishment was up to 12 hours isolation in the refractory ward and an alteration in the diet! However when a young mother was one of the troublemakers she was exempted from punishment as she was breast feeding her baby.

The rules stated that any inmate with a complaint should forward it to the Board of Guardians and represent the case themselves at the fortnightly meetings. An 11 year old boy of a violent disposition was defended by his mother in an unusual manner - she addressed a letter to the Board Chairman and threw it out of the window. She complained that the Master had beaten her son, but on examination it transpired that the boy had been expelled from the Workhouse school for using very indecent language to the girls and since then he had been breaking stone during the usual hours. The Master admitted that he had "administered corporal punishment to him on two or three occasions but only to a proper and moderate extent; and the boy was of so violent a disposition that he had once attempted to strike the Master with a besom". The Board dismissed her complaint. As she repeated her aggressive behaviour later they were probably justified. An imbecile woman charged with deserting her illegitimate children was remanded temporarily in Ross Lock-up House in November 1849 and a few months later she is reported as complaining the Master had punished her unfairly. One malicious inmate accused the Master of giving food to one of the younger women secretly. The Guardians dismissed this, saying his character was unimpeached. He, Mr Smith, reported to one meeting that ----- "the male inmates of the Workhouse had been in the habit of getting out of their yard over the wall into the women's yard". Resolved "Mr Joseph Drew be employed to do what is necessary in preventing any communication between the two yards ---- and also to do what repairs are necessary to the oven".

But the Master's troubles were not over . One of the Guardians ---- "had been informed that some of the female paupers had on several occasions, dressed themselves in men's clothes and got into the men's ward". The informant repeated her story to the visiting committee; on investigation it was verified that this had occurred - "but it appeared that it had been done as a frolic and not with any criminal intent. The men's clothes had been removed from where they were necessarily kept after they are taken off until they are washed". The report continued "The Committee place little or no reliance on the testimony of the witnesses, as to the disgusting acts of immorality which they allege to have taken place but supposing their statements to be true inasmuch as all parties kept the facts from the Master and Mistress no blame is attributable to them and it only proves the very depraved character of the female inmates themselves".

In the years 1838 and 1840, and after the 1870s, Guardians were pressurised by the Central Authority to reduce their grants of out-relief. When this was combined with severe weather, or agricultural depression and loss of employment, the House held more able-bodied, turbulent people. The discipline of the school and the apathy of the infirm ward would have offered a welcome contrast for the overworked Master and Matron.

THE AGED, INFIRM AND SICK POOR

These three classifications of the poor were treated kindly under the 1834 Poor Law Act. Out-relief was always available to them as a means of avoiding destitution and the Workhouse alternative was only offered to them when their living conditions, or state of health, necessitated this. However the out-relief so generously offered was accompanied by vigilant examination of the financial circumstances of their children or relatives, with a view to reimbursing the Poor Rates of their respective Parishes: so much so that many poor people tried to avoid asking for relief for the aged in their families. Medical relief was available to them through personal application to their District Relieving Officer.

The aged and infirm poor, initially described as the 'impotent poor', were those aged over 60; infirm meant those permanently incapable of obtaining paid employment.

The sick poor were not only able to apply for medical relief but could be brought into the Workhouse for treatment and nursing. In 1861 a non-resident pauper, Sarah Gardner who was "bedridden and very ill", was authorised by the Clerk of Westbury-on-Severn Union, where she resided, to be brought to the Ross Workhouse in a fly. Ross Board agreed to bear the expense, and as she came from Walford, that Parish was debited in due course.

When the elderly came in they were able to enjoy some privileges. After an 1847 ruling aged married couples could stay together, if they wished, whereas all other age groups were strictly segregated as regards sex. The aims of the Act had been that inmates of different age groups should also be kept separate, but in most mixed general workhouses, as in Ross, this did not happen. Also the classification was negated by household chores and general tasks, and by the statutory prayers: also, probably, communal meals.

However peace and quiet in the twilight of their lives was not to be enjoyed by the aged in this House! In August 1839 the elderly women complained of the noisy behaviour of the younger women. The committee appointed by the Guardians to investigate the problem presented a most illuminating report. ----- The committee have met -----"to investigate the complaint made to the Board as to the want of proper classification of some of the inmates of the House & of disorderly conduct arising therefrom. These irregularities are wholly confined to the female apartments -----". The report details the accommodation arrangements and continues ----- "it appears that last week there were 20 sleeping in room No 57, viz 14 girls from 9 to 16, 3 women between the ages of 70 and 80 and 3 able bodied women with children [two illegitimate] ------ and there were at the same time 17 sleeping in No 58 viz 7 women with children, 6 of them illegitimate, 2 women whose husbands are in prison [one with an infant child], 1 women deserted by her Husband & 7 other able bodied women one of them [who has since left the House] very much diseased with syphilis. These two rooms are opposite each other with only a narrow landing place between them and the doors being unlocked at night while the inmates were there it follows that between 7 & 8 in the evening and 6 in the morning there is no restraint upon the inmates of these rooms of whatever character or age as they are thus indiscriminately mixed together". The Chaplain, the Rev, Mr Brasier, reported that the two elderly women - ---- "on being called upon with others on Sunday to receive the Sacrament, declined assigning as a reason that they had been so much disturbed by bad language and general confusion in the room that

Reproduced by kind permission of Mrs V J Robbins   c1930s

The Infirmary

they had been unable to prepare themselves for it". The practical solution offered was to close up the doorway of one room , and reopen it at the far end with access to a separate staircase. Also plans to build over the Fever Ward or the Board Room were put forward by the committee.

Some deference was paid to the needs of the aged and infirm - their dietary was slightly more indulgent. A historian of the period reports that the policy of uniformity affected even these few luxuries - "it had been found that the old men and women who were allowed weekly allowances of tea and butter would not take their teas simultaneously or consume their little pats of butter evenly. This distressing deviation from the dietetic uniformity led the Central Authority to suggest the withdrawal of the privilege, in favour of simultaneous service of a certain quantity of liquid tea and of portions of "bread and butter". It is to be hoped that the Master, Mr Henry Smith, did not take up this suggestion. The aged and infirm were set light tasks, such as wood chopping or bundling, hoeing or weeding and sewing, mending and household work for the women. However as cards and all board games were banned the evenings must have been long. The whole routine was regimented with rigid times for meals, rising and going to bed.

From 1895, fortunately for them, the policy changed. This may have been a result of the new ruling as regards Guardians' eligibility for election. Until then they had to be wealthy landowners: from 1895 the more modest landowners could be elected to represent their respective Parishes. [Ross Parish had four Guardians, Walford two and the others one Guardian each]. Also the number of women Guardians increased significantly.

Newspapers came into the House and acknowledgements to the 'Ross Gazette' and 'Man of Ross' are recorded. The Ross Cottage Hospital donated periodicals and in 1901 a library was set up. From 1883 the men over 60 were permitted one day in every two months out of the House, and those over 70 one day in every month without application. Under the strict Poor Law rules the women inmates were only allowed out accompanied. However in 1908 the men's privilege was restricted - only deserving cases enjoyed this temporary freedom.

Most of the rural areas suffered a more stringent ruling under the Outdoor Relief Prohibitory Order [1844 - 1911] as it was those areas that had, in the opinion of the Poor Law Central Authority, misused relief. Also the able-bodied in urban areas could not avoid periods of unemployment as trade and industrial development fluctuated. The strictures of this order in rural areas included the insistence that the wives of able-bodied men, even if ill, had to accompany their husbands into the Workhouse if relief was required

The sick poor received the best treatment available ; cleanliness and discipline were the aim, but some of the nurses employed were erratic in their behaviour, judging from accounts of flirtations with the porters, insubordination with the Master and on one occasion theft from a patient. The sick were, in later years, isolated in the Infirmary - this was separated from the main building in line with central policy. From 1867 the 'outside' sick poor also had greater consideration and care and persons receiving relief on account of temporary sickness were visited fortnightly by the Relieving Officer. National awareness of hygiene and dietary health requirements influenced the regulations affecting workhouses and the infirm and sick were the beneficiaries. Here the extensions in Ross of 1890, brighter rooms, better ventilation, segregation from the younger inmates [in 1908 the old men were removed from the boy's dormitories to their own rooms] and more varied diets were all improvements.

In 1908 with the introduction of Old Age Pensions - 5s.0d per week to all over 70 whose annual income was less than £21. [and Graduated Pension where the total income was between £21 and £31] the elderly were able to escape the stigma of pauperism. Children could afford to maintain their aged parents and, in theory, their numbers in the workhouses should have decreased. In Ross this appears to have been the case -
<u>AgedAdmitted to Ross Workhouse (over 70 years)</u>

1909 - 32   1911 - 24   1912 - 16

The sick poor also benefited; a professional nurse was recruited in 1898 - at a salary of £30 pa with beer allowance, board, lodging, washing and an indoor uniform provided. By a previous Nursing Order no pauper ward attendants were permitted.

One of the essential skills was midwifery. In 1909 a night nurse was needed, as the Infirmary was full. Women in the community began to play a more prominent part. They had always been involved in private charity work and from 1897 joined visiting committees to inspect the home conditions. Later women Assistant Relieving Officers were able to help ameliorate conditions out in the Parishes - a forerunner of the later District Nurse service.

A simple clerical innovation - the Case Paper System - came in generally around 1911. This was a continuous record of each pauper family's history and needs.

Relaxation of the rules, concessions in diet and general improvement in comfort must have made the lives of the aged, infirm and sick more tolerable. Tobacco and snuff were allowed for both sexes and 'dry tea' allowed to the older women. Later cocoa and coffee were added as treats for both sexes in the older age group. Fixed mealtimes were abandoned and cubicles built in the dormitories. Mixed day rooms were introduced and a report in 1914 thanks the proprietors the Ross Picture Palace for "allowing the inmates to attend every Saturday during the year". One Union was granted the right to provide a harmonium, chargeable to the Poor Rates, for the use of the inmates in the workhouse. Here in Ross, the gift of an organ was much appreciated. Mr Rex Roff, the last Master, used to play it in the chapel to accompany the hymn singing.

LUNACY

In contrast to the harsh attitude towards the able-bodied paupers and the vagrants, the New Poor Law Administration dealt kindly with lunatics and the 'feeble minded'. At least 12 Acts regulating their care were enacted between 1774 and 1890. In 1885 Commissions of Lunacy were set up. The vigilant Commissioners caused the Ross Guardians much irritation as they made regular, rigorous inspections of the workhouse.

One of the reports in April, 1873, outlines the conditions :-

"At my visit to this Workhouse today , I saw all those classed here of unsound mind; they are five women, one of whom only was in bed, and but for slight indisposition.

This house is still overcrowded and the means at the disposal of the Master and Matron for securing the personal cleanliness of the inmates inadequate. For 120 inmates of whom 60 are children, there is one portable bath; the only other bath is that in the receiving ward. This necessitates I am told 10 persons being washed weekly in the same water - a most objectionable practice. The house diet, giving only 3 oz of solid meat in 3 days of the week, is too low for persons classed as insane and extra diet should be given to all of them. I learnt that there was no closet for either of the female sick wards. The dress supplied is sufficient - I trust that when the additions to this Workhouse, too long delayed, but now in progress, shall be completed, the imbecile class may be accommodated in the infirmary, as far as possible, that there they may have fixed baths with hot and cold water supply pipes. The bedding which I inspected was clean but under blankets are required. The ground for exercise is, it seems, limited temporarily by the building operations; the imbeciles capable of walking abroad should I think, be frequently taken beyond the premises."

Long before the New Poor Law [1834] each parish had been responsible for its own feeble minded or imbecile parishioners and licensed private houses and, later, County Asylums for the lunatics, were appointed by the Justices and inspected regularly by a physician. Mr Millard's was the nearest licensed asylum to Ross ----- at Portland House, Whitchurch ----- in 1848 he wrote with details : his charge of 12s.0d per week for each pauper lunatic included board, lodging, washing, medicine, medical attendance, attendance of a servant and clothing. Dr Gilliland had a similar establishment in Hereford but after 1851 the patients were removed, with the Relieving Officer, to the newly opened Joint Counties Asylum at Abergavenny. The lunatics are listed, with their removal and maintenance expenses. Occasional cures and discharges are noted and also the deaths.

The cost of maintaining pauper lunatics was repaid by their respective parishes and, where possible, some of this was recouped from their relatives. Monies found on a 'wandering lunatic' - £35.15s.0d - had to go in a separate account, so that all the expenses incurred could be deducted and the balance transferred to common charges to meet his maintenance costs. Two years later the Relieving Officer "put into the hands of the Clerk part of a watch, a chain. a ring and a brooch" - which had belonged to the man : he had since died in the Asylum and had no known relative.

There is very little indication of the lives of the feeble minded living in the Workhouse, but it is known that when they were harmless and physically fit, they did simple household chores and in many cases looked after younger children. They mixed with other inmates despite official pressure to segregate the classes, As late as 1908 two babies were in the care of two imbecile women. The Guardians were not in favour of sending the mentally retarded to Asylums unless their conduct endangered the other inmates, mainly because their maintenance costs at the Asylums were higher than in the House and it was time consuming and often impossible to recover these costs, with the inevitable rise in the charge on the Poor Rates.

In the House, assessments were made - "as to who were supposed to be fit subjects for a lunatic asylum". However, at a later date two Guardians considered that at least ten of the lunatics confined in the various Asylums - "were suitable for treatment in this Workhouse if suitable accommodation could be provided for them". The early policy was that all the sick poor, which included the mentally defective, should be maintained in their own home areas but if any 'persons of unsound mind' found their way to a Workhouse they were to be detained. By legislation a dangerous lunatic could not be detained in a Union Workhouse for more than fourteen days and during that time they had to be examined, segregated and restrained if necessary, before assessment and removal to an asylum. After the establishment of the Lunacy Commission [1855] many lunatics moved out of the Workhouses into the Asylums, but as the Webb's put it - "this was more than made up by the increasing tendency to seclude the village idiot so that the Workhouse population of unsound mind actually increased".

Recorded cases in the House include a man whose noisy behaviour had caused much trouble. A report signed by the Master, Matron, MO and three inmates [two with a cross - 'his mark'] declared that the man's 'mental derangement' was such that finally he had to be strapped to a bed. He was certified by the MO for the House, Mr Edmund Jones, as being of unsound mind "and the accompanying order signed by Wm Bridgeman Esq for his conveyance to the Asylum". But he was sent back on the following morning by Mr Millard who had refused to receive him. The Board requested Mr Millard's attendance and explanation at their next meeting, but he sent a letter instead, it read ; "I hereby certify that the patient's mental faculties are more or less enfeebled from paralysis yet he cannot be deemed insane". A female lunatic who had been very disruptive in the House was sent to the same place and Mr Millard was consulted before she was "enlarged". However she was fortunate - "if she prove not to be a dangerous lunatic the vestry of Walford had reported, through the Chairman, that a meeting of the Ratepayers had been lately held on the subject and that she could be taken care of, if enlarged, at a charge of 5s.0d per week".

In the latter years of the 19th century the number of pauper lunatics increased alarmingly: some were boarded out with relatives or friends. The Hereford County Asylum at Burghill reported that it could not accommodate any more female patients. Later that year, 1895, it was suggested that a mild case in the Asylum belonging to Ross Union could be exchanged for a bad case in the Workhouse. Two upper rooms in the Receiving Ward buildings were prepared with a communicating door to an attendant's room. The nurse was offered 15s.0d per week [with board and lodging] and the Master was authorised to buy a "straight-jacket".

At this time in Burghill Asylum, there were 407 inmates [186 males and 221 females] and of these 53 belonged to Ross Union [24m & 29 f]. The weekly maintenance charge per patient was between 8s.9d and 9s.0½d per week.

The 1901 Commissioners' Report stated that there were 4 men and 9 women imbeciles in the House, and that looped pipes in the WCs had to be cased in to prevent suicides.

Children over 5 years presented a problem if they were mentally retarded. In 1907 an advertisement in the Ross Gazette invited a foster home for a little imbecile girl, with an allowance

J M Briffet   1976
The Vagrants' Ward

allowance of 5s.0d weekly plus 10s.0d a a quarter for her clothing. Sadly, after a month, Daisy was sent back to the Workhouse. In 1904 a Royal Commission recommended that all mentally defective persons should be taken out of the Poor Law administration and placed under the direction of the Lunacy Authority Councils. The Act of 1913 placed this duty upon County Councils. Separate institutions for the different categories was the aim, but the War intervened and only the urgent cases were removed. An authority on the subject estimates the national numbers in 1914, as 1% of the whole population, 'between 400,000 and 500,000 of either sex, of all ages, the great majority of them being at some period in their lives, either in receipt of poor relief or nearly destitute - and it is estimated that the feeble minded still constitute at least one fourth of the total inmates of the workhouses'.

VAGRANCY

The newly built Union Workhouses provided convenient 'bed and breakfast' stops for the casual poor or vagrants. No out-relief was to be given to this class of pauper but they had to be admitted to the

Workhouse if they were in real need. The Central Authority policy was strict with vagrants all through this period, although greater concern developed for the health and comfort of the other classes of pauper as time went on. Deterrence was the aim: they were to be accommodated in basic lodging houses, or in separate wards in the workhouse. A bath on entry was compulsory, there were no fires in their wards; smoking and card playing was forbidden and their bedding was to be 'inferior' to that of the inmates - "coarse straw or cocoa fibre in a loose tick". Their diet was restricted. Above all they had to complete a task before being released. The tasks varied with age, sex and health of the vagrant, but they were alike in being tedious. Oakum picking was one: oakum was tarred old rope, delivered unbeaten or beaten, ['junk' in the Minutes]. The picked product was sold for caulking ship decks and boards. Chopping wood, pumping water and gardening were other tasks. Stone breaking was the major work, and the tramp cells had sieves through which the occupant had to push his broken stones before he could leave.

The first record of a vagrant arriving is described in Minute Book 2, on 23rd November, 1840 -
"Daniel Burke states that on Thursday the 5th Inst. he went into a Shed in the Parish of Goodrich - there he remained till 4 o'clock the next evening (Friday) when some Woman came to him and gave him some refreshment, he then remained in the same Shed till 4 o'clock the next evening (Saturday) when some Gentleman came to him & gave him in charge of the Constable who took him to a Magistrate, from thence to a Beer house, gave him some Beer, then took him home, afterwards turned him out of his house, he that night slept in a Shed near the Constables with two Pigs. The Constable took him into his house the next morning (Sunday) where he remained till Tuesday evening when he was brought to the Workhouse in a Wheelbarrow covered with a Cider hair - it rained all the way to Ross".

The Constable's action was justified by the fact that the vagrant was paralysed and he judged that - "the Pauper would be less shaken in a Barrow than in a cart or a small wagon".

Inside of Vagrant's Cell at Dore Workhouse
By Kind permission of Ewyas Harold WEA Study Group

Mr Henry Smith, the Master had the duty of relieving the Wayfaring Poor "in and at" the workhouse door. In October 1848 a 'wayfaring woman whose name was unknown' was given refuge as she was very ill. On recovery she wanted to leave but was 'kept to obtain the opinion of the Board', although the House medical officer judged that she was not a "proper subject for a lunatic asylum". The Minute continues - "on her appearance before them the Guardians ascertained that she was a Welch woman and not able to speak but little English --- and having expressed her great distress at being kept in the House the Board told the Master there were no reasons to detain her in the House against her will".

Possibly through overcrowding in the House John Halford, Relieving Officer for Ross, was directed to select a "barn or some convenient and suitable place near Ross to place vagrants & wayfarers applying for lodgings --- and to provide straw to be placed therein and employ a person to cleanse the same from time to time". Two houses in Brampton Street were rented from Mr Richard Jackson, for 2s.0d per week . In 1856 a letter is recorded complaining about the use of Black Lion Court - Malthouse --- for the use of vagrants. The following year the owner, Mrs Brewer, gave the Board notice to quit and the Clerk was asked to enquire whether premises at the top of Corpse Cross St. could be "letted". The lessee John Partridge said they could have the remainder of his term, but the owner, Mr Davis, objected to this sub-let "for the purpose contemplated" --- back to Mrs Brewer's premises, at a weekly rental of 3s.0d house, [the RO for vagrants was, at this time, also paid 3s.0d per week].

In 1862 the Board considered that "a considerably greater number of vagrants were relieved in this Union than in any neighbouring Unions" and recruited the Superintendent Constable, Charles

Hopton, stationed in Ross, as Assistant Relieving Officer for vagrants at a salary of £5 per annum. After examination, if the vagrant was considered eligible for relief, he would be given a ticket — this entitled "the applicant to a night's lodging in the vagrant ward and 1 lb of bread from the Union Workhouse on the following morning" — 3 months later the Board reduced the bread allowance to ½lb. A system of passes, or tickets, issued by neighbouring Unions was tried, with the incentive that vagrants producing such a pass could have 8 oz bread: those that did not 4 oz. But the system failed - the Tramp Master's Book "showed that less than 5% of vagrants relieved in the Ross Union had come with 'Way Tickets' " [Feb 1869].

The new Workhouse extension of 1872/3 included male and female vagrant wards, with six hammocks for "one half of the male wards and the female wards to be supplied with bedsteads". In March 1874 the wards were ready for occupation and, in line with the local Government Board's rule, placards were printed and placed in each ward — "stating the task of work required to be performed also the Diet to be allowed to the different classes of tramps". The Ross 'visitors' were ingenious. A Minute in 1874 requests tenders from local ironmongers —" for the alteration of the stone screens, the spaces at present being so wide that an arm may be put through and fastenings tampered with and also that the tramps are enabled to push large stones through the openings instead of breaking them", Messrs Perkins and Bellamy's tender, at 3s.9d per screen was accepted. At this time able-bodied vagrants were required to break 5 cwt of stone each for one night's stay. In April 1883 the edict went out — the task of work for a vagrant detained during the day was to be increased to 8 cwt of gravel. A Minute, a few months later, reported the Clerk's return showing a considerable reduction in "vagrants' admission and nights lodgings".

There are records of stone being delivered to the house by local suppliers and in 1879 the Guardians had a large surplus of broken stone, which they sold to the Highway Board at 4s.0d per yard, also "the Highway Board to be asked to provide, deliver and stack at the workhouse all the stone required for breaking by the Paupers and Tramps and to pay the Guardians 1s.6d per yard for breaking such stone— ".

Female tramps and children were normally accommodated in the lodging houses, and the women given tasks of oakum picking. This unpleasant work had been prohibited for female convicts in prisons in 1896, but a Poor Law Conference Report of 1900 noted that "many country Masters expect female tramps to pick 2lb of unbeaten oakum and keep them prisoner until it is done".

The rise in vagrancy between 1847 and 1848 was repeated in 1895 and 1910. Responsibility for all Poor Law administration was taken over by other Departments by 1907, — except for the continuing deterrent regime for vagrants exercised by the Boards of Guardians. The anomaly was they were solely concerned with their own Union's needs and the tramps, wayfarers or men looking for employment were itinerants. Only by discouraging their stay in the Workhouse could savings be made on the rates. Thus local and national statistics must be doubtful as they do not record the many people sleeping rough, but without 'tasks' !

In 1911 new Tramp wards were built on the Union House land: the porter's salary was increased by £2.10s per annum and he was given a uniform, which the Guardian's Committee considered would give him more authority. The Police were no longer required to assist and the Master was, in recognition of his added work, also given an allowance of £10 per annum.

An analysis of the average number of inmates in the house in 1913 and 1914 shows little change, ie 1913 - 91 and 1914 - 89, but the average number of casuals relieved in Ross per fortnight changed dramatically in the last 4 months of 1914.

	Jan-Aug	Sep-Dec
1913	227	180
1914	160	87

The Clerk noted, on 26th November 1914 - "No casual applied for admission on Tuesday last. A most unusual occurrence."

There was a general reduction in poverty helped by the Welfare Reforms from 1910. During World War 1 vagrancy almost disappeared as Army Service, or vacancies in unskilled jobs provided opportunities for work. These Ross statistics reflect this national trend. Sadly, after 1948, vagrancy and poverty returned.

REFLECTIONS

It is difficult to summarise the many aspects of the New Poor Law and its effects in the Ross Union.

The policy of the Central Authority was, initially, aimed at discouraging the poor of all classes from seeking relief. Thus the Workhouse functioned as a deterrent for the helpless paupers as much as for the underpaid and unemployed poor.

Fortunately the Ross Guardians, along with many other Boards of Guardians, appeared to have been more lenient towards the poor for whom they were responsible. Over time, nationally, the system became less rigid: contemporary criticism and up-to-date anlysis are reflected in the following quotations:-

"I consider the Workhouse as now organised is a reproach and disgrace peculiar to England: nothing corresponding to it is to be found throughout Europe."

Robert Pashley (1805-1859) Barrister and QC. Author of 'Pauperism and Poor Laws'. pub 1852. Longman, Brown Green, & Longman, London.

"There was to be one institution in each union for all classes of pauper. It was to be a place which, whilst it provided the full requirements of physical welfare, starved both the will and intelligence, and forced the pauper into a condition of blank mindedness."

p 82 ENGLISH POOR LAW POLICY by Sidney and Beatrice Webb. First published 1910

"The New Poor Law Administration was a combination of Victorian free market economics, with a vast bureaucratic machine of government; with all this, however, all this Victorian corporatism, the edifice was baffled by its own paupers".

Summary from talk given at Course on 'Poverty and Poor Law', School of Continuing Studies University of Birmingham Sep 1994.

Any inaccuracies in this study are entirely the responsibility of the authors.

REFERENCES

1. Records of Clerk to the Guardians
    Minute Books - 1836 -1914   HRO Ref No : K42/406 - K42/428
    Minute Books of Finance Committee : 1905 - 1914   HRO Ref No : K42/434 - K42/435
    Minute Books of House Committee : 1905 - 1914   HRO Ref No : K42/439 - K42/440

2. The Ross Gazette

3. Report by the Royal Commission on the Historical Monuments of England (1992/1994)

4. Ross Vestry Minutes L78/8

5. "Poor Relief in Hereford with Special Reference
        to the first 15 years of the Hereford Union 1836 - 1851" by Sylvia A Morrill (1972)

6. "Ross Union 1836 - 1857" by C John Powell (1972)

7. Bagley JJ & AJ The English Poor Laws London (1966)

8. M A Crowther The Workhouse System 1834 - 1929 Methuen, London (1981)

9. Dr Anne Digby Pauper Palaces Routledge & Kegan Paul, London (1978)

10. Morris M H The Book of Ross-on-Wye Barracuda Books, Buckingham (1980)

11. Webb S & B   English Poor Law History Vols 1 & 2 (first published 1929)
                 English Poor Law Policy (first published 1910)
                          [Part of a series on ENGLISH LOCAL GOVERNMENT]
                 Frank Cass & Co Ltd, London (1910)

RECOMMENDED BIBLIOGRAPHY

1. Anstruther, Ian The Scandal of the Andover Workhouse Geoffrey Bles, London (1973)

2. Englander, David Poverty and Poor Law Reform in 19th Century Britain 1834 - 1914
        from Chadwick to Booth   Addison-Wesley, Longman (1998)

3. Longmate, Norman The Workhouse Temple, London (1974)

ACKNOWLEDGEMENTS

Photographs on pp 12, 16 & 17 are reproduced by kind permission of Mrs V J Robbins of Weston-under-Penyard.

The Photograph on p22 is reproduced by kind permission of the Ewyas Harold, WEA Study Group and is on p11 of their publication 'Dore Workhouse in Victorian Times' - Author, Nancy Elliott pub 1984.

Extracts from the Ross Union Minute Books are reproduced by kind permission of Herefordshire Council.

Appendix A

Parishes	Guardians elected	Names of Guardians qualified to act in the Parish where no Guardian have been elected
Ballingham		Clement Cade
Brampton Abbotts	Daniel Dew	
Bridstow	William Wylie	
Brockhampton		William Stallard
Foy		William Jones.
Goodrich	Thomas Powell	
Harewood	Charles Andrews	
Hentland	Thomas Meats	
Hope Mansell	Cornelius Morfell	
How Caple	John A Hollings	
Kings Caple		James Price
Llandinabo	Richard Howells	
Llangarren	Geo Woodall Lloyd / Frederick Price	
Llanwarne	George T Taylor	
Lea Bailey	Cornelius Morfell	
Lea Gloucester		
Lea Hereford	John Lodge	
Marstow		Thomas Barnett
Pencoyd		
Peterstow	Revd W Coke	
	William Dew	
	Wm Cary Cocks	
Ross	Joseph Pearce	
	Thomas Morfell	
	William Bonnor	
Ruardean	John Vaughan	
St Weonards	W V Foxwell	
Sellack	Thomas Dew	
Sollershope	Joseph Till	
Tretire	Frederick Price	
Upton Bishop	Henry Chellingworth	
	Thomas S Braddock	
Walford	Isaac Theyer	
Weston	William Bennett	
Yatton	William Gibson Ward	

The Ross Union Guardians by Parish in 1861

Tradesmens a/c for the quarter ending Michs last

Joseph Turnock	Beer &c	£5. 1. 0
Richard Parker	Butcher	37. 4. 9
John Wellington	Wine & Spirits	3. 15. 6
John C Bonner	Milk	7. 19. 2
Edward Wood	Barm	11. 2. 0
William Meek	Coals	11. 14. 3
William Watkins	Currier	5. 2. 2
John Williams	Boots &	28. 0. 0
Atkinson & Co.	Drapers	11. 14. 9
William Blake	Ironmongery	1. 15. 0
William Preece	Blacksmith	3. 1. 6
John Phipps	Pump Maker	1. 5. 1
Messrs. Smith & Wood		10. 9. 5
Edwin Deeley	Draper	3. 5. 8
Benjamin Brunsdon		34. 17. 10

Henry Minett to pay

William Newton	0. 2. 9	
Thomas Robinson	0. 14. 0	
Walter Morris	0. 11. 10	
Charles Morgan	0. 7. 0	
Sam Hurst	0. 10. 3	
Joseph Drew	0. 17. 4	
James Cotton	0. 13. 10	
William Henry Morris	0. 13. 4	4. 10. 4

Tradesmens' Accounts for the Ross Union in October, 1862

506

...penditure for the Half year ending Lady-day 1866.

Parishes	In-maintenance (88)	Out-relief & Non-resident (89.90.91 & 100)	Vaccination (118)	Registration (119)	County Rate (120)	Funerals (116)	Visiting Lunatics (115)	Other Charges	Common Charges (114)	Balance in Favor (129)	Balance against
llingham	13.9.10	11.16.4	.	.5.6	7.7.2	.	.	.	25.15.6	13.2.1¾	.
mpton Abbotts	.	19.1.½	.	.9.6	18.13.-	.	.5.	.	57.7.9	33.6.5½	.
dstow	18.16.2	56.10.5	.7.6	1.4.9	30.8.6	.	.	.	102.15.6	16.13.2½	.
ckhampton	.	.	.	.3.9	8.18.6	.	.	.	22.15.5	12.14.3	.
	19.15.1½	38.-.6½	.	.8.3	24.17.-	.	.	.	73.19.6	40.19.1¾	.
odrich	2.5.1½	50.5.1	.	1.3.9	32.15.6	.	.	.	87.8.4	82.-.10¼	.
arewood	.	.	.	.2.	6.2.2	.	.	.	21.2.6	11.-.2½	.
entland	13.9.10	46.10.3	.7.6	1.9.6	33.6.6	.	.	.	93.10.6	96.9.6¼	.
ope Mansell	1.2.4	1.18.3	.17.6	.8.3	12.4.6	1.9.6	.	.	35.18.5	29.6.11¼	.
w Caple	3.7.5	14.19.2	.	.6.3	10.8.-	.	.	.	30.14.8	13.11.7	.
ngs Caple	.2.9	38.7.10	.	1.8.3	24.3.8	.	.	.	71.17.10	46.3.11½	.
ndinabo	.	8.-.3½	.2.6	.1.	5.6.-	.	.	.	16.8.3	15.14.4	.
langarren	13.7.6	152.7.-	.	1.18.	54.8.-	.	.2.6	.	169.19.2	123.8.2	.
anwarne	5.16.-	41.13.5	.	.16.	17.6.2	.	.	.	65.8.5	52.12.3¾	.
a Bailey	.1.2	10.14.3	.	.4.3	4.8.-	.	.	.	7.17.6	2.3.11½	.
a Gloster	.	.	.	.3.	2.-.-	.	.	.	6.18.9	8.12.1½	.
a Hereford	3.7.5	3.14.7	.	.1.	6.8.2	.	.	.	20.19.4	4.12.10¼	.
arstow	.	1.16.-	.	.2.	10.4.8	.	.	.	28.15.11	14.9.9¼	.
ncoyd	.	5.12.3	.	.5.	11.16.2	.	.	.	30.11.6	42.4.2½	.
terstow	30.11.8	13.18.3½	.15.-	.12.6	19.6.6	.	.	.	59.11.9	17.16.2	.
fs	66.5.6	267.6.5	3.6.-	8.15.	122.-.-	.	.10.	.	351.13.3	241.15.2	.
uardean	.8.11	54.3.2	.5.-	1.9.3	37.16.3	.	.10.	.	58.15.6	58.17.6¾	.
t Weonards	6.5.3½	84.2.5	.	1.2.6	30.15.8	.	.	.	111.11.2	92.16.11½	.
llack	3.7.5½	31.4.2	.	.17.3	19.7.8	.	.	.	55.18.9	62.19.10	.
llershope	.	26.5.1	.	.8.3	7.9.6	.	.	.	23.-.6	31.15.11	.
tire	2.19.-	5.19.½	.	.3.	11.4.-	.	.2.6	.	143.17.6	44.6.1½	.
lton Bishop	6.3.9	91.13.½	.	1.5.3	31.12.4	.	.10.	.	92.13.2	60.18.2½	.
alford	8.14.3	142.2.11	2.-.-	1.18.9	47.14.4	1.1.9	.10.	.	134.12.4	181.-.4¼	.
eston under Penyard	5.6.5	64.-.5½	1.17.6	1.7.9	51.-.-	.	.15.	.	141.17.9	72.15.½	.
atton	12.5.11	32.16.4	.	.14.9	10.18.-	.	.	.	38.9.10	13.11.4	.
TOTALS £	237.8.10	1341.13.6	9.18.6	29.14.3	710.14.11	2.11.3	3.5.0		2082.6.3	1557.18.9	

...xamined 6th June, 1866.
C. Merrill?, Auditor

J. Stanley Power, Chairman,

Statement of Expenditure by Parish in 1866

19 MAR 1914

Cordwood, at 8/6 per		Mr R. Jones
Firewood, at 27/8 per 1,000 Bundles.		Messrs S. Llewellyn & Son
Do	Loose at 1/10 per Cwt.	Do
Do	Blocks at 9ᵈ per Cwt.	Do
Coffins, at prices quoted.		Mr J. L. Hiller
Boots & Shoes,	Do	Messrs E. Turner & Co. Ltd.
Repairs to Boots &c.,	Do	Messrs Watkins & Cox
Conveyances, at 6ᵈ per mile each way.		Mr. G. Baynham
Clothing, at prices quoted		Messrs Johns & Sons.
Garden Seeds,	Do	Messrs J. H. Davies & Sons
Drapery,	Do	Messrs Southall & Son.
Milk, at 9½ per gallon.		Mr W. R. Beavan.
	For 6 Months.	
Meat.	Beef at 9ᵈ per lb	Mr J. Maddocks.
Do	Joints at 10ᵈ	Do
Do	Mutton at 8½	Do
Do	Suet at 3ᵈ	Do
Bread.	at 3¾ᵈ per 4 lb. loaf.	Mr Percy Jones.
Flour	at 26/6 per sack.	Do
Cake	at 3ᵈ per lb.	Do
Coal & Coke	at prices quoted.	Messrs Webb, Hall & Webb, Ltd.
Groceries	Do	Messrs J. Barnwell & Son.
Soaps &c.	Do	Do
Brooms &c.	Do	Do
Tinned Goods.	Do	Messrs Chamberlain & Arnold.

It was moved by Mr. J. Murdoch seconded by Mr G. W. Jones and resolved that the report of the Committee be adopted.

Traders who Supplied the Ross Union in 1914

PINK PUBLICATIONS

No 1   **WALTER SCOTT'S CHARITY SCHOOL,**
ROSS-ON-WYE
by Kevin Brookes & Colin D Price
1993

No 2   **THE LIME KILNS AND ASSOCIATED QUARRIES**
IN WALFORD, ROSS-ON-WYE
by C A Virginia Morgan
1993

No 3   **A HISTORY OF THE RIVER CROSSING AT**
WILTON-ON-WYE, HEREFORDSHIRE
by Heather Hurley
1993

No 4   **A HISTORY OF THE MANOR OF WILTON**
AND PARISH OF BRIDSTOW
by R A Hart
1994

No 5   **A LANDSCAPE HISTORY OF GANAREW,**
HEREFORDSHIRE
by M A Howard
1994

No 6   **THE KNIGHTS TEMPLARS AND HOSPITALLERS IN**
THE MANOR OF GARWAY, HEREFORDSHIRE
1086 - 1540
by Joan Fleming-Yates
1995

No 7   **NATHANIEL MORGAN 1775-1854**
OF ROSS-ON-WYE, HEREFORDSHIRE
by C A Virginia Morgan
1995

No 8   **THOMAS BLAKE 1825-1901**
THE PIOUS BENEFACTOR OF ROSS-ON-WYE
HEREFORDSHIRE
by Jon Hurley
1996

No 9   **HISTORIC HAREWOOD**
HEREFORDSHIRE
by Heather Hurley
1996

No 10   **RIVER ROAD AND RAIL**
in
THE MONNOW VALLEY
by Joan Fleming-Yates
1997

No 11   **THE ROSS UNION WORKHOUSE**
by C A Virginia Morgan and Joyce M Briffett
1998

OTHER PUBLICATIONS

THE ROSS-ON-WYE WALKABOUT LEAFLET

ISBN   0-9532021-0-0